THE FINANCIALLY INFORMED INVESTOR

It's what you don't know
that could potentially
cost you a bundle.

Jim E. Sloan

Six-Time Author

Printed in the United States of America

ISBN 978-0-578-73105-6

Book cover design by Cathi Stevenson
www.bookcoverexpress.com

Self-published August 2020

Available in print or on Kindle at
www.amazon.com

DISCLAIMER

Investment advisory services offered only by duly registered individuals through AE Wealth Management, LLC (AEWM). AEWM and Jim Sloan & Associates, LLC are not affiliated companies.

Investing involves risk, including the potential loss of principal. No investment strategy can guarantee a profit or protect against loss in periods of declining values. None of the information contained in this book shall constitute an offer to sell or solicit any offer to buy a security or any insurance product.

Any references to protection benefits, safety, security or steady and reliable income streams in this book refer only to fixed insurance products. They do not refer, in any way, to securities or investment advisory products. Annuity guarantees are backed by the financial strength and claims-paying ability of the issuing insurance company. Annuities are insurance products that may be subject to fees, surrender charges and holding periods which vary by insurance company. Annuities are not FDIC insured.

The information and opinions contained in this book are provided by the author and has been obtained from sources believed to be reliable, but accuracy and completeness cannot be guaranteed. They are given for informational purposes only and are not a solicitation to buy or sell any of the products mentioned. This book is not intended to be used as the sole basis for financial decisions, nor should it be construed as advice designed to meet the particular needs of an individual's situation.

Jim E. Sloan and Jim Sloan & Associates, LLC does not give tax or legal advice. The firm is not affiliated with the U.S. government or any governmental agency. Hypothetical examples have been provided for illustrative purposes only; they do not represent a real life scenario and should not be construed as advice designed to meet the particular needs of an individual's situation. A Roth Conversion is a taxable event and may have several tax related consequences. Be sure to consult with a qualified tax advisor before making any decisions regarding your IRA. 00544205

TABLE OF CONTENTS

CHAPTER ONE

What is your decision-making process when making major financial decisions?

Over the years, I've found that the average investor and many sophisticated investors, typically don't have a process to filter out myths, misconceptions and missing information, and I have encountered many that were making major financial decisions based on emotion, opinions, and missing information, rather than facts, logic, and math.

A thorough process should include asking the right questions, getting the relevant facts on the table, running some math calculations, and analyzing the results for the best possible outcome.

The following are some of the answers I've heard over the years when asking common questions pertaining to major financial decisions that many investors make:

1. What age should you begin SSI?

   Answer: *"I'm going to begin as early as possible because it probably won't be there for my lifetime."*

   Answer: *"I'm going to wait until full retirement age to begin."*

   Answer: *"I won't need the income, so I'll wait until age 70 and allow my benefit to grow."*

2. Do you have a written budget so that we know how much income to solve for each month?

   Answer: *"No, but I'd say I need about $6,000-$7,000 per month."*

   Answer: *"Yes, here is my monthly household budget sheet."*

3. To provide for your income in retirement, which accounts will you draw from first?

   Answer: *"I'll probably withdraw from my savings and mutual fund accounts first."*

   Answer: *"I'll deplete my IRAs first, then my after-tax accounts last."*

   Answer: *"I really don't know."*

4. I see that you have the majority of your assets invested in pre-tax accounts such as your 401k and IRA, and nothing in a Roth IRA. How did you arrive at your decision to save on a pre-tax basis?

   Answer: *"I like the tax-deduction I get on my contributions."*

   Answer: *"That's what my CPA tells me to do each year to reduce my tax liability."*

5. When you're done using your money (at death), what would the tax impact look like for your family when they inherit?

Answer: *"Honestly, it doesn't matter, let them pay the taxes. It's more than I received when my parents died."*

Answer: *"I don't know, I haven't looked into that."*

These are just a few basic financial questions that many investors are unsure of how to arrive at the optimal conclusion for their situation. Having a process in place could help avoid making decisions that could result in a substantial negative impact on the outcome of any financial plan.

I believe an investor should gather the relevant facts pertaining to the issues and put them on the table, which then allows for decisions to be based on facts, logic, and math, rather than emotions and missing information.

Hopefully, this book will become a catalyst for you to do just that. Become informed!

CHAPTER TWO

Know your math

What if you knew the right questions to ask and had the capability to run the math regarding the financial decisions you're facing, wouldn't it become easier to arrive at a better possible outcome?

Although there are many scenarios I could run, in this Chapter, we will focus on five major financial decisions that investors typically face as they age.

1. What is the optimal age to begin Social Security—age 62, 66, 70...or somewhere in-between?
2. What is the optimal order of withdrawal from your accounts in retirement? Should you draw down pre-tax or after-tax accounts first? Does it matter?

3. Over time, should you convert some of your pre-tax money in 401k plans and IRAs to an after-tax account such as a Roth IRA or other tax-free growth vehicles?
4. How would potential future long-term care expenses for one or both retirees affect your retirement funds and income streams? Where would the money come from, to pay that first bill?
5. Once retired, could you sustain your current standard of living into and through retirement?

To begin determining the best possible outcome, our firm bases each scenario on the amount of retirement funds and income you're projected to have through age 100. We could use a different age, perhaps 85, 90 or 95 if someone has major health issues or a family history of short life expectancy.

These two statistics[1] from the U.S. Census Bureau shines a spotlight on the graying of America. Not everyone will live a long life, but many will.

1 https://www.census.gov/library/publications/2020/demo/p25-1144.html

- The nation's age 65+ population is projected to nearly double in size in coming decades, from 49 million in 2016 to nearly 95 million by 2060.
- The nation's age 85+ population is projected to nearly double in by 2040, from 6.4 million to 14.4 million, and nearly triple by 2060 to 19 million.

Let's review and better understand the potential impact of common, major financial decisions that pre-retirees and retirees are making every day. I will introduce five hypothetical families that each have a specific concern and run a current and projected analysis for each, then review possible outcomes.

Disclaimer for all scenarios: The projections and calculations used in this Chapter are for illustrative purposes only. Projections are based on information such as estimated Social Security benefits, pension benefits, projections of cost of living increases, inflation rates, and federal and state income tax rates. Current federal income tax tables are used in certain calculations, which are subject to change and could affect the long-range outcome shown. Interest rate assumptions are hypothetical and are not meant to represent any specific investment. Thomas Gold Solutions, LLC has done the due diligence to maintain the accuracy of the calculations and outcomes, but the assumptions do not encompass all situations.

Jim Sloan & Associates, LLC and Thomas Gold Solutions, LLC do not make any guarantees on the outcome of any recommendations made based upon these hypothetical scenarios. The projections or other information generated by the analysis regarding the likelihood of various investment outcomes are hypothetical in nature, do not reflect actual investment results, and are not guarantees of future results.

Hypothetical assumptions for all scenarios:

- Income and expenses to increase 2.25% annually for inflation
- Investments are projected to grow at 5% annually, net of fees and expenses.
- Assume current tax rate of 22% and remains unchanged for their lifetime.
- Scenarios will be run to age 100 unless specified differently.

Case Study #1: Your Household Budget

Having an accurate accounting of your monthly and annual household budget should be the foundation of every retirement income plan. Without a solid foundation, your retirement dreams and expectations could be altered substantially, solely based on missing information or misinformation.

I have encountered situations where a family estimated the amount of annual income that they will need in retirement based on what they're spending today, and believe that is what they will need, or close to it. If we take that amount and inflate annually over a 25-30-40 year retirement, that could falsely necessitate solving for more income than is needed.

In some instances, so much more income, that someone might think they will never have enough to retire or would run out of money prematurely.

Hypothetical Case Study: Andy and Angie Applesauce, married, ages 63 and 61 with three children.

In lieu of providing an itemized household budget, they decided to estimate their monthly income needs because they had a good idea of what they spend monthly. They indicated their need to be $7,500/monthly spendable income at retirement.

Details:

- Current Monthly Income: $8,500 gross (assume 22% tax-bracket)
- Current Monthly Expenses: $7,500 net
- Retirement Monthly Expenses: $7,500 net
- Retirement Monthly Income Needed: $7,500 net
- Total Retirement Funds: $754,000 gross
- Angie wants to begin SSI at her full retirement age (66 and 8 months)
- Andy wants to begin SSI at his full retirement age (66 and 2 months)

- Angie begins her pension at age 65: $1,800 gross monthly

Goals:

- Angie plans to retire in 3.5 years
- Andy plans to retire in 2 years

Current Scenario: I entered the data they provided along with their goals and ran a scenario to see if they would run out of money before age 100.

The results of Current Scenario:

Year	Client Age	Spouse Age	Retirement Funds
2040	82	85	$187,242
2041	83	86	$104,032
2042	84	87	$12,127
2043	85	88	$0

Analysis: Under these assumptions, the Applesauce's are projected to deplete their retirement funds at ages 85/88. This is exactly what we do not want to see. Could we move the gray line out further into the future or get rid of it altogether?

My first recommendation would be to ask them to complete a monthly budget worksheet and let's discover what their budget really looks like. Do they really need the $7,500 net monthly income forever?

After they completed my budget worksheet, it became apparent that they did not need $7,500 net monthly. Their revised and accurate monthly budget came in at $5,735 net monthly needed for the next 10 years, afterward, their income needs drop by another $1,700 monthly due to paying off their mortgage.

That is a huge difference between solving for $7,500 net monthly income forever instead of $5,735 net monthly income for the next 10 years, then $1,700 less than that monthly, for the remainder of their lives.

Let's see what the new projections look like with the revised budget.

Scenario with Revised Budget: Using the revised data that was provided on their budget worksheet and running another scenario, could we move the gray line out into the future or eliminate it altogether?

The results of the Revised Scenario:

Year	Client Age	Spouse Age	Retirement Funds
2055	97	100	$1,023,440
2056	98	101	$997,081
2057	99	102	$968,655
2058	100	103	$938,387

Analysis: The results of their revised scenario is exactly what we want to see. Instead of running out of money at ages 85/88, the Applesauce's now are projected to have **$938,387** in retirement funds through age 100/103.

Before you begin thinking that's magic. Not at all, it's math.

It's simple math:

$7,500 net monthly initial need. $5,735 net monthly revised need = $1,765 net monthly not needed x 37 years = **$783,660** income not needed to solve for.

Completing a budget worksheet helps us realize that the expenses we have today will change as we move forward in life. Health care most likely will rise continuously, but most other expenses may reduce or go away altogether as we age.

This scenario is an example of how important it is to know your budget and not just throw out a number, because that could give you a false reading about your long-term financial health.

Know your math. Become informed!

Case Study #2: What is your optimal age to begin Social Security?

The optimal age to begin Social Security income is dependent on various factors. If you have limited resources and assets, and need the income, it may be best for you to begin as soon as you can. Under current law, that age is 62. If on the other hand, you have sufficient resources and assets to rely on, then delaying could be the optimal strategy to help improve your overall financial outcome.

Let me illustrate by using another hypothetical family, Bob and Betty Blueberry.

Hypothetical Case Study: Bob and Betty Blueberry, ages 59/58, would like to retire at ages 63/62 and have one child.

Details:

- Combined Monthly Income: $9,500 gross (assume 22% tax-bracket)
- Current Monthly Expenses: $5,000 net
- Total Retirement Funds: $653,000 gross

- They both retire and begin SSI at age 65
- Bob begins $1,900 mo. pension at age 64

Scenario #1: I entered the data that they provided along with their desired ages to begin Social Security income and here is what we discovered.

The results of Scenario #1:

Year	Client Age	Spouse Age	Retirement Funds
2059	99	98	$836,280
2060	100	99	$788,766
2061	101	100	$737,113
2062	102	101	$681,183

Analysis: Under these assumptions, they are projected to have **$788,766** in retirement funds at ages 99/100. Can we improve this outcome?

Scenario #2: We adjusted 3 pieces of data. We have them working another 2 years, delaying their SSI until full retirement age of 67 each, and had Bob delay his pension until age 65.

The results of Scenario #2:

Year	Client Age	Spouse Age	Retirement Funds
2059	99	98	$1,257,662
2060	100	99	$1,214,097
2061	101	100	$1,166,550
2062	102	101	$1,115,104

Analysis: Under these assumptions, the Blueberry's are projected to have **$1,214,097** in retirement funds at ages 99/100. That is an additional **$425,331** we uncovered.

The Blueberry's have choices now. It was important for them to discover the optimal age to retire, begin Social Security and not run out of money.

This scenario illustrates the importance of running the math when making major financial decisions, instead of having an idea of when you want to retire and hope it works.

Case Study #3: What is your optimal withdrawal order?

In retirement, income is typically derived from pensions, Social Security, pre-tax and after-tax accounts. Have you ever wondered which accounts should be drawn down first? It may not sound like a big deal, but it could be.

Scenario #1: This hypothetical family, Charlie and Cindy Cranberry want to know if it's better for them to withdraw from their after-tax accounts or pre-tax accounts first? Or does it matter?

Remember, after-tax accounts typically are taxed on the growth only and pre-tax accounts are taxed on the entire amount withdrawn.

Hypothetical Case Study: Charlie and Cindy Cranberry, both age 63, Cindy is retired, and Charlie wants to retire in 4 years at age 67. No children.

Details:

- Charlie's Monthly Income: $10,000 gross (assume 22% tax-bracket)
- Current Monthly Expenses: $6,200 net
- Total Retirement Funds: $808,000 total ($58K Savings, $350K After-Tax, $400K Pre-Tax)

Scenario #1: Let's illustrate the outcome if the Cranberry's withdrew from their after-tax accounts first and the pre-tax accounts last.

The results of Scenario #1:

Year	Client Age	Spouse Age	Retirement Funds
2054	97	98	$781,731
2055	98	99	$714,862
2056	99	100	$641,103
2057	100	101	$560,224

Analysis: Under these assumptions, if the Cranberry's drew down the after-tax accounts first, they are projected to have **$641,103** in retirement funds at ages 99/100.

Scenario #2: Now, let's illustrate the outcome if the Cranberry's withdrew from their pre-tax accounts first and the after-tax accounts last.

The results of Scenario #2:

Year	Client Age	Spouse Age	Retirement Funds
2054	97	98	$844,980
2055	98	99	$781,165
2056	99	100	$710,539
2057	100	101	$632,678

Analysis: Under these assumptions, they are projected to have **$710,539** in retirement funds at ages 99/100. If they withdraw from their pre-tax accounts first, they are projected to have an extra **$69,436** in retirement funds at ages 99/100.

The order in which you draw down your retirement accounts is one of many important decisions that you will want to evaluate. Become informed!

Case Study #4: Should you convert some of your IRA/401k plan to a Roth IRA?

There are two ways to save for retirement, either on a pre-tax or after-tax basis. Saving in a traditional IRA, 401k plan, 403b plan or 457 plan would generate a tax-deduction in the year of your contribution. The tradeoff is that in return for your up-front deduction, all contributions and growth are taxable at time of withdrawal.

By saving in an after-tax account like a Roth 401k plan or Roth IRA for example, you forgo the up-front deduction, but your contributions and growth would be tax-free upon withdrawal.

Over the years, I've heard the following as to various reasons that some have chosen to save pre-tax over after-tax;

"I like the tax deduction because it helps keep my current tax bill low."

"I'll be in a lower tax bracket when I retire, so it makes sense to get the deduction now."

"I really don't know other than my CPA tells me that is the way to keep my taxes as low as possible this year."

I understand where these responses are coming from and they might make sense if you are just looking at what you could do this year to minimize your tax bill, which is what the CPA is trying to help you with, then I get it. That is the micro view (annual tax picture). We take a macro view (lifetime tax picture).

What we have are investors saving for their future and trying to make the best decisions that they can, without having the facts and figures on the table. Has anyone run the math for you?

There are two types of scenarios. The first is for those that remain in the workforce and are contributing to their retirement accounts. Should you continue saving pre-tax or after-tax, or a combination of the two?

The second scenario we find are those that are near retirement or already retired with large pre-tax accounts. Do you leave those accounts as-is and draw down as needed or required in retirement? Or, do you consider a partial Roth conversion from pre-tax to after-tax? Let the math tell us the optimal path.

Hypothetical Case Study: The next hypothetical family, Dan and Daisy Dewberry, ages 66/62, both recently retired and have two children.

Details:

- Combined Monthly Income: $7,800 gross (assume 22% tax-bracket)
- Current Monthly Expenses: $6,200 net
- Total Retirement Funds: $1,530,000 gross
- Dan begins $2,100 mo. pension at age 67
- Both begin SSI at age 70

Scenario #1: Run scenario with no Roth IRA conversion.

The results of Scenario #1:

Year	Client Age	Spouse Age	Retirement Funds
2055	101	97	$3,022,050
2056	102	98	$3,057,858
2057	103	99	$3,094,272
2058	104	100	$3,131,950

Analysis: Under these assumptions, the Dewberry's are projected to have **$3,022,050** in retirement funds at ages 97/101. Not bad.

Scenario #2: Now, let's see if we can better their outcome by converting $250,000 IRA money over 5 years into a Roth IRA.

Here are the results of Scenario #2:

Year	Client Age	Spouse Age	Retirement Funds
2055	101	97	$3,099,196
2056	102	98	$3,137,876
2057	103	99	$3,174,437
2058	104	100	$3,208,934

Analysis: Under these assumptions, the Dewberry's are projected to have **$3,099,196** in retirement funds at ages 97/101. This scenario projects **$77,146** more in retirement funds at ages 97/101, showing us that a partial Roth conversion does provide the Dewberry's with the optimal outcome.

Scenario #3: Now, let's see if we can better their outcome even further by converting $500,000 IRA money over 5 years into a Roth IRA.

Here are the results of Scenario #3:

Year	Client Age	Spouse Age	Retirement Funds
2055	101	97	$2,743,403
2056	102	98	$2,763,702
2057	103	99	$2,804,144
2058	104	100	$2,853,157

Analysis: Under these assumptions, the Dewberry's are projected to have **$2,743,403** in retirement funds at ages 97/101. This scenario projects **$355,793** less in retirement funds at ages 97/101, showing us that a $500,000 partial Roth conversion is not the optimal path.

There are some financial professionals that tout taxes are on sale today and you better hurry and convert as much of your forever taxed accounts (pre-tax) to never-taxed accounts (tax-free). That sounds good in theory and could make sense in some instances, however, without running the math, it's impossible to know if that would be the best outcome for you.

Case Study #5: How would your retirement portfolio withstand a long-term care event?

In Chapter 6, I discuss long-term care planning, so I'll keep this brief. Many mature investors understand the value of protecting their retirement portfolio against potential future long-term care expenses, and then decide against insuring that risk after getting a quote for long-term care insurance.

They might say *"it's too expensive"* or *"they will raise my rates"* or *"what if I don't use it?"*

"It's too expensive?" Let's hypothetically say that you paid **$80,000** in premiums over the next 25 years for a LTC policy with **$500,000** in tax-free LTC benefits.

Hypothetically, the first day of year 26, you or your spouse (if married) have a long-term care event and now you need home health care for years, typically provided by a spouse, child, or friend.

One day, it becomes too much for them to handle and you move into an Assisted Living Facility, stay there three years, and then move to a nursing home for the last year of life.

For this example, let's assume your spouse, child or friend provided your home health care, at no cost to you. You will begin to pay the total cost of the four years of long-term care expenses as I've laid it out above and that would be potentially **$500,000** after-tax dollars needed.

If you are self-pay (no insurance), then you would pay the **$500,000** out of pocket. That's **$500,000** tax-free dollars you'll withdraw from your retirement portfolio over a 4-year period. You'll pay $1.00 for every $1.00 of care needed.

Insure the risk? Let's hypothetically say that you bought a long-term care insurance policy instead of self-insuring. You pay **$80,000** in premiums over 25 years and this policy provides **$500,000** in tax-free long-term care benefits.

Let's examine the math. **$500,000** in LTC benefits divided by **$80,000** premiums paid over 25 years **= 0.16¢** per tax-free dollar that you bought, to be used for LTC expenses.

If you and/or your spouse never have a long-term care event, maybe you might regret buying the insurance. However, if you have a care event that lasts for a period of time, the financial impact to the sustainability of your portfolio could be disrupted in a big way.

"They will raise my rates." Not so fast. While there is no guarantee of a rate increase, Colorado is among 40 states that enacted regulation to combat that issue.[2] Colorado residents purchasing long-term care insurance today are protected by Colorado's Rate Stability Regulation. The regulation has helped curb long-term care insurance rate increases in Colorado because it forces long-term care insurance companies to lower their profits if they seek a rate increase.

2 AARP Public Policy Institute August 2018, page 5.

"What if I don't use it?" What if you did? Would you prefer to protect your portfolio and never have used it...or have a major heart attack or stroke later in life so that you can use it? I say that tongue in cheek, but the main reason people buy insurance is to cover the risk of something important to them, in this case, you're protecting your portfolio from being depleted due to an unexpected LTC event.

Let's run a scenario to analyze what a long-term care event might look like for someone that is insured versus someone that is uninsured and self-pays.

Hypothetical Case Study: Our last family is Eddie and Edith Eagleton, ages 62/63, both recently retired with four children.

Details:

- Combined Monthly Income: $6,200 gross (assume 22% tax-bracket)
- Current Monthly Expenses: $5,400 net

- Eddie begins SSI at age 64: $2,100 monthly
- Edith begins SSI at age 64: $1,485
- Edith begins pension at age 64: $680 monthly
- Total Retirement Funds: $766,000 gross

Scenario #1: Run scenario with neither ever experiencing a long-term care event.

The results of Scenario #1:

Year	Client Age	Spouse Age	Retirement Funds
2055	97	98	$668,334
2056	98	99	$652,437
2057	99	100	$633,142
2058	100	101	$609,848

Analysis: Under these assumptions, the Eagleton's are projected to have **$633,142** in retirement funds at ages 99/100. Looking good.

Scenario #2: Now, let's analyze how the portfolio would respond if Eddie experienced a long-term care event at age 84, lasting 4 years, then passes away at age 88.

The results of Scenario #2:

Year	Client Age	Spouse Age	Retirement Funds
2042	84	85	$777,875
2043	85	86	$552,291
2044	86	87	$292,835
2045	87	88	$0

Analysis: Under these assumptions, the Eagleton's are projected to have a gray line and run out of money at age 87/88. Why? Because they self-paid four years of care for Eddie at ages 84-88. I discuss this in length in Chapter 6, but to get an estimate of what care costs in 20-25 years, you should take the costs today and inflate by 4-5% annually until time of utilization. I use 4% in my scenarios. This once healthy portfolio has been disrupted in a big way.

Scenario #3: Now, we'll analyze how the portfolio would react if Eddie experienced a long-term care event at age 84 and it lasts 4 years, but they have a long-term care insurance policy to cover those potential expenses. Over 25 years, the Eagleton's paid **$80,000** in premiums for Eddie's long-term care policy. Once he enters a facility, no further premiums are due.

The results of Scenario #3:

Year	Client Age	Spouse Age	Retirement Funds
2055	97	98	$423,923
2056	98	99	$395,521
2057	99	100	$363,082
2058	100	101	$325,971

Analysis: Under these assumptions, the Eagleton's are projected to have **$363,082** in retirement funds at ages 99/100. Having a long-term care insurance policy to cover the costs for a care event is the difference between the Eagleton's running out of money at age 87/88 and having **$363,082** in retirement funds at age 99/100. Know your math.

Chapter Summary: As you have seen throughout this Chapter, if you go about life making major financial decisions based on misinformation, missing information, and without important math calculations, you could end up with a financial outcome that may not be optimal.

Become informed. A good place to begin is to take 10 minutes and discover for yourself what your basic financial analysis could look like through age 100, at no cost to you.

From the comfort of your home or office, you could visit **www.jimsloan.com**, click on the orange ***Retirement Analyzer*** button and enter 9 bits of basic contact and financial information. This will allow you to generate your own basic analysis, edit it, and run as many scenarios as you want. If you don't like the outcome or have questions after you run your basic analysis, I'm available to answer your questions by email which is **jim@jimsloan.com**.

To run your own basic financial analysis today, visit: **www.jimsloan.com** and click on the orange ***Retirement Analyzer*** button.

CHAPTER THREE

What is your optimal age to begin Social Security?

When should you begin Social Security benefits... age 62, 66, 70 or somewhere in-between? This is a question that many boomers are asking and if you guess wrong, it could be an irreversible mistake that may cost you many thousands of dollars in lost income over your and your family's lifetime.

This Chapter is designed to help you understand the various ages that you could begin receiving your Social Security benefits, some advantages and disadvantages of each, along with four different ways that could help you increase your benefits.

You could visit the Social Security Administration website (www.ssa.gov), learn the rules and your projected benefits at various ages, however that is just the beginning of the process.

I have discovered that good planning requires someone helping you understand the long-term consequences of the decisions that you make today. There is no one-size-fits-all answer pertaining to when you should begin collecting your benefits. It all depends on your particular situation.

For example, someone beginning early benefits at age 62 and living into their 90's, could end up leaving many thousands of dollars on the table. Saying that, it still might make sense for some to claim early benefits if they are not working and have limited resources.

On the other hand, if someone is still working, claiming early benefits may not be optimal, because they may lose some or all of their benefits until they attain full retirement age.

To help determine the optimal age to begin your Social Security benefits, it is recommended that you have a financial advisor run various scenarios, beginning at different ages and incorporate with your overall retirement income plan. This process allows you to view various ages to begin your benefits.

It then becomes fairly easy to select the age that gives your best potential outcome. Know your math.

The following questions are helpful when deciding on when to begin collecting your Social Security benefits:

1. Other than SSI, what other sources of income will you have?
2. How much of the other income is taxable?
3. How much do you have in savings and investments?
4. Are you working now, and if so, when do you want to retire?
5. Are you married, and if so, when will your spouse be retiring?

6. If married, is your spouse retired or retiring from an employer that does not pay into Social Security?
7. How is your health and do you have longevity in your family?
8. There are additional questions, but you get the idea. The answers are necessary to help you make informed decisions on optimizing your Social Security benefits.

Are there ways to increase your Social Security benefits?

Yes, there are four ways that might increase your Social Security benefits.

1. Work longer, earn more.

Your earnings record for Social Security continues to be updated as long as you work and pay into Social Security. If you keep working at a relatively high salary, it can cause one of your lower-earning years to drop off the 35-year earnings record and serve to boost your primary insurance amount (PIA). Your PIA is also known as your monthly SSI benefit amount. This advice is especially important for people who do not have 35 years of high earnings, such as women who have stayed home to raise children.

It even applies to high earners in their 50s and 60s; although the earnings in their early years are indexed for inflation, the indexed amount is likely lower than their current salary.

A person with 35 years of maximum earnings can continue to improve their earnings record by replacing one or more of those early indexed years with today's higher earnings.

2. Delay applying for benefits.

After attaining full retirement age, if you decide to delay receiving SSI benefits, under current law, your benefit increases by 8% annually until age 70, at which time, there is no further advantage of delaying your benefits.

In a low-return environment, those 8% annual delayed credits that an unclaimed benefit earns between the ages of 66 and 70, could end up being quite valuable.

3. Maximize survivor benefits.

A unique benefit for married couples is that when one spouse dies, the surviving spouse would receive the higher benefit of the two.

Hypothetically, let's say Jack and Jill are married.

Jack dies while receiving a benefit of $2,000 monthly. Jill's $1,000 monthly primary benefit will change to a $2,000 monthly survivor benefit.

One way to maximize the survivor benefit is to have the high earner delay benefits to age 70. This could maximize their joint income while both spouses are alive, and it will maximize the surviving spouse's income after one spouse dies.

An important note is that applying before full retirement age could be problematic for a high wage-earner, even if he or she is not expected to live very long.

For example, Jack applies for Social Security at age 62 and dies after receiving three checks. In this case Jill's survivor benefit will be based on Jack's age 62 benefit. However, if he dies without having applied for Social Security, her survivor benefit would be based on his full retirement age benefit, which could be up to 30% higher.

4. Keep more of your Social Security benefits by reducing or eliminating taxes.

Once you begin receiving your Social Security benefits, you will fall into one of three categories of taxation—either none of your benefits will be taxed, 50% will be taxed, or 85% will be taxed. The amount of Social Security benefits that are taxable depend on how much 'provisional income' you have for the year.

Three steps for calculating 'provisional income': Begin with your gross income...

1. Add any tax-free interest you received, such as interest from a municipal bond
2. Add 50% of your Social Security income to that figure.

Example: Let's say your gross income is $25,000 and you earned $2,500 in municipal bond interest. Add those amounts together to arrive at $27,500. Now let's assume you receive $24,000 in Social Security benefits. Half of that is $12,000. Add these together and you have a 'provisional income' of $39,500.

0% Taxable: If your 'provisional income' is $32,000 or less, and you file a joint return, your Social Security benefits are federal income tax-free.

If your 'provisional income' is $25,000 or less, and you file single or head of household, your Social Security benefits are federal income tax-free.

50% Taxable: If your 'provisional income' is between $32,001 and $44,000, and you file a joint return, up to 50% of your Social Security benefits would be taxable.

If your 'provisional income' is between $25,001 and $34,000, and you file single or head of household, up to 50% of your Social Security would be taxable.

85% Taxable: If your 'provisional income' is above $44,000, and you file a joint return, up to 85% of your Social Security benefits would be taxable.

If your 'provisional income' is above $34,000, and you file single or head of household, up to 85% of your Social Security benefits would be taxable.

Can you reduce or eliminate Social Security taxation altogether?

In some instances, I've seen taxpayers reduce their 'provisional income' to where their SSI benefit is taxed slightly or not at all. These people only had after-tax accounts. If your investment income is derived mostly from IRAs, then that income is generally 100% taxable, making it more difficult to get under the 'provisional income' threshold where your SSI benefits are tax-free.

If your income is derived from after-tax accounts, only the interest earnings are taxable. So, you could potentially receive the same amount of income, but a smaller percentage of the income would be taxable (interest earnings). By doing this, your 'provisional income' could be reduced to below the threshold at which your Social Security income is completely tax-free.

When should you begin receiving your Social Security benefits?

To determine your optimal age to begin your Social Security benefits, it is recommended that you meet with a financial advisor that will take the time to understand your situation and run the math. Only then, could you have the necessary information to make an informed decision not only about what age to begin Social Security, but also how this decision affects your overall retirement income plan.

If you don't have an advisor or would like a second opinion, you can reach me at jim@jimsloan.com.

CHAPTER FOUR

Do you have a *Structured Income Plan* for your retirement years?

One of the biggest risks to a typical retirement portfolio, is the stock market performing negatively or taking a nose-dive in the early years of retirement. That could cause an impact that may not be recoverable for some. We refer to this as the 'Sequence of Returns' risk.

The risk is this: Most would agree that the stock market is designed to grow long-term. We don't know from year to year, if the market will be up or down. And if your retirement plan includes withdrawing income from investment accounts that are going through a down cycle or a volatile period, that could become an issue. That is the 'Sequence of Returns' risk, not knowing the returns you'll receive year to year.

Invest for the long-term, right?

Investment institutions across the land educate investors to invest in stock and bond portfolios for the long-term. They say, the further we're away from retirement, to allocate a larger percentage toward equities and a smaller percentage in bonds. As we get closer to or in retirement, they say to reallocate to less equity holdings and increase bond positions.

That's it? It's that simple, huh. What if I need income on day one of retirement and my portfolio is in negative territory for the year and the market is quite volatile? My portfolio is losing value and you say to withdraw my income anyway. Isn't that the opposite of what we've been taught about buying low and selling high?

The issue is that retirees need income this year, and next year and the next. Will the stock market be up when you retire and need income? Or down?

Somehow, the 'Sequence of Returns' risk seem to be ignored. Being primarily invested in stocks and bonds are great when you have years for your accounts to grow and overcome short-term dips and corrections in the markets. However, when you need to rely on these investments to generate income early on in retirement, that's when problems tend to emerge.

If the markets zoom up during your first few years of retirement, consider yourself fortunate and most likely avoided the 'Sequence of Returns' risk. If on the other hand, the markets are negative early on in your retirement years, that could spell trouble for your retirement income plan.

It's important to ensure that you not only have a retirement income plan, but the plan is structured in such a way, that can help mitigate the 'Sequence of Returns' risk.

Our firm utilizes a *Structured Income Plan* to help our clients avoid this risk. Essentially, we split client assets into multiple buckets and assign job descriptions to those buckets. I didn't invent the bucket strategy, but it is quite effective.

Here is an example of a *Structured Income Plan:*

BUCKET #1: This bucket is designed to provide the client with dependable and predictable income during the first five years of retirement. We typically utilize low risk or protected savings vehicles that are designed to achieve this goal. Savings, CDs, Treasuries, certain types of bonds, and income annuities are options to help achieve this bucket's goal.

BUCKET #2: This bucket is designed to grow for five years and then provide income for the next five years. We could use bonds or fixed annuities with income riders that are designed to help achieve this bucket's goal.

BUCKET #3: Given that we have just addressed the first 10 years of income in retirement, with low or no stock market risk, this bucket's job description is to grow for 10 years then provide income. We could utilize a wide variety of securities instruments in this bucket and allow these investments the potential to perform over a long period of time while mitigating client emotions of short-term volatility inherent when invested in the market. It also helps clients avoid 'knee-jerk' reactions of wanting to go to cash during volatile times.

BUCKET #4: Given that we have just addressed the first 15 years of income in retirement, this bucket's job description is to grow for 15 years then provide income. Similar to bucket #3, we could utilize a wide variety of securities instruments in this bucket and allow these investments the potential to perform over a long period of time while mitigating client emotions of short-term volatility inherent when invested in the market. It also helps clients avoid 'knee-jerk' reactions of wanting to go to cash during volatile times.

I've illustrated four buckets to describe a *Structured Income Plan*. There are times where we may use 5-6-7 buckets. The purpose of this strategy is to generate income without subjecting the first 10 years of income to market volatility. Structured income planning provides the client with income while allowing the stock market to do what it does long-term, thus helping to avoid the 'Sequence of Returns' risk.

CHAPTER FIVE

The Tax-Deferred Disconnect

In 23 years of helping investors with major financial decisions, I have witnessed disconnects in the wealth management and financial planning area, with the largest one primarily income-tax related.

In this Chapter, I'll discuss two disconnects relating to the tax-deferred wealth inside annuities and pre-tax retirement accounts such as 401k plans, 403b plans and IRAs.

Disconnect #1: Tax-deferred wealth inside annuities

According to the Investment Company Institute[3], as of March 31, 2020, there were $2.2 trillion dollars in this country, in tax-deferred wealth inside of annuity contracts, either variable

3 https://www.ici.org/research/stats/retirement/ret_20_q1

annuities, index annuities, fixed annuities or immediate annuities.

Annuities are tax-deferred savings vehicles that are typically purchased to be used for income at some future point. What if an annuity owner ends up not needing those dollars for income after-all and are inherited by the next generation?

Many times, we have consumers acquiring an asset believing that they are going to use it for retirement income, but that annuity is never needed to supplement their income and it ends up going to their beneficiary. If the beneficiary happens to be children of the deceased annuity owner, what could that look like?

If the children are successful to any degree, some of them could be in a modest to high tax bracket. So, what we have is a 60-70-80 year old person that might be in a modest or low tax bracket today, growing tax deferred wealth and never spending those dollars. If those annuities aren't depleted by the owner and the children inherit them while in a modest to high tax-bracket, the children could end up with a significant tax bill that may have been avoided or reduced with proper discovery and planning.

The disconnect as I see it in the wealth advisory and financial planning community is that some financial professionals primarily are accumulating assets, managing money, implementing diversification strategies, but are not necessarily asking the discovery questions surrounding their clients tax-deferred money.

What are the tax implications on tax-deferred annuities being inherited by someone else? Has anyone run the math for you? Who will be paying the taxes on the growth inside of these annuities and what could that look like?

For the annuity owners that won't need those dollars for income, further discovery and additional planning should be considered. There are strategies and techniques available to either reduce that problem or completely eliminate it, if we catch it early enough.

Disconnect #2: Tax-deferred wealth inside pre-tax retirement accounts, such as 401k plans, 403b plans, and IRAs.

According to the Investment Company Institute[4], as of March 31, 2020, there were $17.4 trillion dollars in pre-tax accounts such as 401k plans, 403b plans, and IRAs.

What I've witnessed is that some upper middle class, higher net worth investors reach age 72 and are required to begin IRA minimum distributions for the remainder of their lifetime. Some have told me that they don't need the income and don't want to take it out because they don't want to pay more taxes. Sorry, that's not an option. Unless you want to face a 50% penalty on the amount you were supposed to withdraw and didn't, you might want to withdraw your minimum distribution annually.

I've seen either one of two things take place. They withdraw the money, pay the taxes and deposit into their savings account to earn bank rates forever or they invest in another tax-deferred or

4 https://www.ici.org/research/stats/retirement/ret_20_q1

on-going taxable account. By doing the latter, they are either increasing their own taxation each year or deferring and growing an additional tax bill for their heirs.

There are different types of strategies and techniques available to either leverage that required minimum distribution into something that would replace the lost tax dollars to their beneficiaries or children rather than just have that become a cost every single year.

This tax-deferred disconnect is one that you and your children could possibly face. What about you? Are you in line to inherit your parent's tax-deferred wealth? What tax bracket are you in today and what would your tax bill look like upon inheriting those accounts?

You may be a 55-65 year old successful business owner or individual that has a 85-90 year old parent about ready to drop a $500,000 IRA in your lap.

I have found that this tax-deferred wealth issue is rarely discussed. We all assume that our financial professional, our CPA, and our estate planning attorney are aware of the issue and it has been taken care of. If that were so, I wouldn't be using any space in this book discussing this looming and often overlooked issue for tax-deferred wealth owners.

I've spoken to many CPAs over the years and the common response I've heard was that they knew this was a problem, they see it, but they didn't think there was anything that could be done about it.

I shared with them, that it really isn't their job to solve the issue, instead uncover it so that they could bring someone like me in to have further discovery on the issue. That's where we would run an analysis for the CPA's client and deliver the report to the CPA. Become informed and know your math.

You do have a choice

When you begin to withdraw money from your tax-deferred accounts in retirement, every dollar will be taxed at your marginal tax rate at that time? And it should be the highest taxed asset you own because all withdrawals will be taxed as ordinary income, which means it goes on top of your other income.

Unless donated to a charity, a reasonable person should expect to pay taxes over the lifetime of their pre-tax retirement accounts, beginning with their first withdrawal. The issue is not that you'll pay taxes on these accounts. The issue I'd like to draw your attention to, is the failure to run the math on your projected lifetime tax liability on these accounts. Using conservative projections, it's eye-opening to see how large an account could become in 25-30-40 years. What does your lifetime projected tax bill look like and is there anything you can do to mitigate it?

Hypothetical example: Let's say that Greg, age A65 has a $500,000 IRA that under normal circumstances, doesn't need and won't be spending. His wife Gayle is age 64 and they have two children.

At age 72, Greg will begin his required minimum distributions and pay the taxes due each year. Because of low bank savings rates, he decides to invest those dollars in another taxable account, which increases their tax bill, not lowering it.

At age 80, Greg passes away and his wife Gayle, at age 79, inherits his pre-tax retirement account. Because this account is not needed for income, she continues the required minimum distributions until she passes away at age 90.

Since Gayle is only withdrawing the required minimum distributions each year until her death, and we assume the account continues to grow for 11 years until her death, the $500,000 IRA she inherited should be a higher value pre-tax retirement account that their two children will inherit.

Eleven years later, the children inherit this IRA. Hypothetically, let's assume that even after the annual required distributions were taken, the IRA grew to $650,000 over the 11 years while Gayle owned it.

Now, the children inherit the IRA and split evenly. They each have $325,000 to either take as a lump sum or withdraw over a maximum of 10 years.

What if they have built successful careers and are already in a modest to high tax-bracket? It doesn't matter, they will have to report the withdrawals on their tax return and that most likely could cause their tax bill to increase.

Side note: On 1/1/2020, the Secure Act was implemented and eliminated the ability of most non-spouse inheritors of pre-tax retirement accounts to spread out the tax bill over their lifetimes. The pre-tax retirement accounts are now required to be depleted within 10 years.

As I've mentioned earlier, paying the taxes is not the issue, it's not running the math to see what that looks like, and to evaluate possible solutions to mitigate those taxes.

Thinking outside of the box

If you won't need the money, why not consider gifting to your favorite charity rather than to the IRS. This way, your favorite charity receives your $500,000 IRA with zero tax due because they are a 501(c)3 non-profit charity.

If you have children, then you could replace the $500,000 fully taxable inheritance to them with a $500,000 tax-free inheritance. To do this, you could withdraw an amount annually from your pre-tax account, pay the taxes and buy a life insurance policy equal to what you gave away, $500,000. Since life insurance is generally paid tax-free to the beneficiary, your children would receive a $500,000 inheritance tax-free instead of being a $500,000 inheritance that is fully taxable. Where did the IRA go? To your favorite charity or charities, tax-free.

Running the math is a valid way to determine the optimal course of action for anyone in this situation. The calculation would include the current and future projected tax liability, the cost of the life insurance coverage and the insurability of the account owner.

A hypothetical conversation might sound like this:

Greg and Gayle, I see that you have $500,000 in this IRA. I also see that you live comfortably on your pension and your Social Security income. You both have long-term care coverage and you've said that you won't be using this $500,000, it'll just go to the children. Greg and Gayle, your parents lived into their 90's and you two could live another 20-30 years. Let's say that your $500,000 account today grows at 3 or 4 percent per year for the next 20-30 years, this account could become a million and a half dollars. Do you realize that's over a million and half dollars of taxable income? Should we have a discovery session to analyze that issue?

Part of the disconnect is when we don't realize that we could be handing our children a Form 1099 for a million and a half dollars, at a 40-50 percent potential tax rate when dumped on top of their current income.

Another part of the disconnect is that insurance regulators tell insurance agents that they can't give tax or legal advice. Securities regulators tell financial advisors that they can't give tax or legal advice. CPAs are not allowed to give financial or legal advice and attorneys are not allowed to give financial or tax advice. The consumer is best served when their financial, legal, and tax professionals work together to meet all of the clients' needs.

You do have a choice. Instead of just accepting this issue as being status quo, what if you could give away the income tax problem to a charity and help build a new wing on a cancer hospital or fund 20 scholarships for disadvantaged children? What if your children could inherit tax-free dollars... instead of fully taxed dollars? What if we could utilize insurance planning to leverage those potential lost tax dollars that you and your heirs are going to pay anyway.

My advice for those that have large pre-tax retirement accounts is to seek out a trusted advisor with experience in IRA distribution planning for further discovery and planning. If you don't have an advisor or would like a second opinion, email me at jim@jimsloan.com and I will be glad to help answer your questions.

CHAPTER SIX

What is your plan when your health fails?

Aging is part of the human life cycle and the purpose of this Chapter is to remind us that if we live the full human life cycle, we will become frail and need daily assistance from someone at some point in our future. And, we may need that assistance for many months or years at home before assisted-living or nursing home care becomes a consideration.

If you are reading this book, most likely you are not in need of long-term care services today. On one hand, that is good because you're most likely healthy, and on the other hand it's bad because the costs for this type of care continues to rise each year.

Let's assume you that won't need care for another 20-25-30 years. What will the cost for services be at your point of need? How would that affect your retirement portfolio? And, do you have a plan in place to help offset or pay for those costs?

Aging Population Explosion

These two statistics[5] from the U.S. Census Bureau shines a spotlight on the graying of America. Not everyone will live a long life, but many will.

- The nation's age 65+population is projected to nearly double in size in coming decades, from 49 million in 2016 to nearly 95 million by 2060.
- The nation's age 85+ population is projected to more than double by 2040, from 6.4 million to 14.4 million, and nearly triple by 2060 to 19 million.

We are living longer due to technology, medical science advancements, and medicine. Will everyone live a long life? Of course not, but as

5 https://www.census.gov/library/publications/2020/demo/p25-1144.html

you can see by the Bureau's projections, by 2060, one out of four Americans will be over the age 65.

My Children Will Take Care of Me

I've heard plenty of times that *"my children will take care of me."* And, they probably will. However, have you walked through that scenario with them?

Does it mean that they will move in with you or will you move in with them and their family?

Does it mean that they will provide hands-on care such as bathing and dressing you?

Or does it mean that they will provide for you financially?

What would the impact be on your adult child's life if they unexpectedly became responsible for your care 24 hours every day for months or years?

What would the consequences be, if they provided care only a few hours a day? What would that do to their family time? To their career? To their other responsibilities and commitments? What would it mean to them financially?

When a long-term care event happens, it is an event that disrupts not only the life of the one needing care, but everyone else is in their life.

Inform Your Loved Ones

Inform your loved ones of your care preferences and have it in writing. Do you want to stay in your current area if you need care or would you move to another part of the country where you have family?

Would you want to receive care at home for as long as possible, or would you prefer to be in a setting such as an Assisted Living Facility where there are other aging people around, where there is help as needed, and there are a variety of social activities planned?

If care is needed, how will you pay for it? You have three choices: Medicaid, long-term care insurance or paying 100% out of pocket.

Some care policies will pay for a caregiver to come into your home to provide care for you, informally (family or friends) or formally (professionals).

You can also insure just a portion of your care costs if you can afford to pay the remaining portion of those costs. This is one reason that having a long-term-care plan is so important. It addresses these issues long before care might be needed.

Financial Consequences:

So how do we begin to plan for living a long life? It starts with being as physically and financially fit as possible.

From a financial standpoint, one concern of many retirees is outliving their assets. Many are reluctant to tap into their principal, wanting to preserve it at all costs. They want to preserve the income stream but also want to preserve the principal so that they have something to leave to their children, grandchildren, or favorite charity.

In my experience, one key risk to an investment portfolio is that of a long-term care event to one or both spouses, if married. As the likelihood of needing care increases with increased age, the long-term care risk to an investment portfolio becomes larger, not smaller, as we age.

Paying for care could disrupt every financial, tax or legal plan that you have in place. For many, paying for care causes a reallocation of resources, starting with income. The issue is that many successful retirees live on most of their income as they did during their working years. Shifting income to pay for care most likely would have a direct impact on the client's ability to keep financial commitments.

These outcomes may include:

- Maintaining lifestyle expenses, including hobbies
- Helping a child who has not made the best decisions in life
- Providing for a child or grandchild with special needs
- Gifting or making charitable contributions

Although in theory, many of these expenses may be considered 'discretionary', in the world of a successful retiree, they are 'nondiscretionary.' Requiring your income to pay for care and cover lifestyle expenses could become a big strain on your retirement funds.

Assets in a portfolio are really capital in nature, that is, the asset's purpose is not to be used to pay for care or any other expense in life, but to generate predictable streams of income that will keep up with a rising cost of living and that the client cannot outlive. The assets' job description is to generate income.

Using capital to pay for care could create unintended issues with:

- Unnecessary taxes
- Market timing
- Liquidity issues
- Leaving a legacy

And perhaps most importantly, every dollar used to pay for care is one dollar less available to generate income to keep future commitments. For the less affluent, using assets to pay for care could start a financial death spiral. Assuming that the majority of assets are used to generate income, here is what could happen:

Year 1: The client tries to continue covering expenses with income generated by assets, while also paying for care from them. If care is paid from qualified or low cost-basis assets, a tax is incurred. The sale of assets are subject to market conditions and if you need to sell, will the values be up or down at that time?

Year 2: Since there are now fewer assets to generate income, more assets have to be used to make up the difference. Of course, those assets are subject to the same taxes and market conditions. This is on top of the additional assets needed to pay for care.

Year 3: See year 2.

Year 4: See year 3.

In fact, this is *exactly* what clients are concerned about when they tell their financial advisors, *"I want to avoid going into my principal."* Paying for extended care will likely force a reallocation of both income and assets. The problem is that none of the money was ever meant to pay for care, which means using it could disrupt every plan you created to secure financial independence during retirement.

A long-term care plan could help alleviate these issues. I don't believe everyone needs long-term care insurance, but I do believe that everyone needs a long-term care plan.

What will it cost for long-term care services when you need it?

The average cost of long-term care services will vary depending on what region of the country where you live or decide to retire. Since the author lives in the Denver, Colorado area, we will use that region to illustrate the typical average monthly costs associated with the different types of long-term care services today.

To learn about the costs in the area where you live, visit Genworth Life's webpage listed at the bottom of the page.

The 2019 Denver area average monthly long-term care costs are:

LTC Services Provided	**Monthly Cost**[6]
Adult Day Care	$1,625
Assisted Living Facility	$4,500
Homemaker Services	$5,577
Home Health Aide	$5,625

6 2019 Genworth Cost of Care Survey www.genworth.com/aging-and-you/finances/cost-of-care.html

Nursing Home (semi-private)	$8,760
Nursing Home (private)	$9,779

To get a fair snapshot of what long-term care costs are expected to be when you might need care, take the above figures and increase by 5% annually (for inflation) until you reach age 80-85.

That is the approximate amount of monthly benefits you'll want to solve for. Then, determine how much of that cost you could pay out of pocket and consider insuring the remainder.
I say approximate amount because we don't know how quick medical costs will rise going forward. However, we do know that the U.S. Consumer Price Index[7] through November 2019 tells us that medical services increased 5.1% over the past year.

For my example illustration below, I will use 5% annual inflation increase, with the understanding that it could be higher or lower.

7 https://www.bls.gov/news.release/cpi.nr0.htm

EXAMPLE: Susan is age 60, lives in Denver and the average monthly cost to live in an Assisted Living Facility (ALF) in 2019 is **$4,500**/month.

Let's assume Susan receives free in-home care from her child for a few years in her late 70's until it is decided that it be best to move into an Assisted Living Facility (ALF) at age 80.

Now, let's take the monthly **$4,500**/month ALF figure today and inflate it at 5% annually for 20 years. The **$4,500**/monthly cost today becomes a **$11,940**/monthly cost when Susan reaches 80 and hypothetically would need care.

Said another way, it will cost **$143,268** annually after taxes for Susan to enter an ALF in 20 years. Let's assume she stays there for 3 years and then enters a nursing home. After entering a nursing home, she passes away one year later.

Here's the math:

$143,268 x 3 years for the ALF = **$429,804**

$322,884 would be the approximate cost for 1 year of semi-private nursing home care at her age 83. ($8,760/month today increased by 5% annually for 23 years).

The 4 years of care in this hypothetical example totals **$752,688** of net income that Susan could need for her care.

Medicaid may provide a limited amount of this type of care to those with low income or minimal resources and assets. The typical reader of this book most likely would have significant assets that they are wanting to protect from future long-term care expenses.

What is your plan to pay for your care?

Whether or not Susan needs **$250,000** or **$400,000** or **$700,000** for her potential future care, the point is that due to inflation and rising costs in health care, what seems like large long-term care costs today become very large costs as the years go by.

Wouldn't you agree that if not planned for, a long-term care event could disrupt any financial, tax, or legal plan you have in place?

That is the *first reason* to begin the long-term care conversation in your early 50's to early 60's. The later you wait, the more expensive it becomes.

The *second reason* is that as we age, our bodies start breaking down, so the later you wait, insurability becomes a factor if your plan includes insurance.

Could you protect your retirement assets and income if you or your spouse, partner, or both, were to need long-term care services for an extended period?

Take a moment and refer back to Chapter 2 and read Case Study #5, to see an example of how someone could pay pennies on the dollar for long-term care insurance.

Hopefully, you and your financial advisor have discussed this topic, so that you have a plan in place the day your health fails? That conversation could be the first step to mitigate the impact that a long-term care event could have on your investment and income plan.

Hopefully, this book will become a catalyst for you to take the first step in your long-term care planning, which is to begin that discussion today and end with a well thought-out and designed plan of action, so that your family is protected and prepared as possible when that day arrives.

Remember, everyone doesn't need long-term care insurance, but everyone should have a long-term care plan.

My advice is to have this discussion with your family and advisor today so that you have a plan for that day. If you do not have an advisor or would like a second opinion, you can reach me at jim@jimsloan.com.

GOT 10 MINUTES?

Discover how far your nest egg will take you in retirement... in just 10 minutes!

Access our ***Retirement Analyzer***, a quick and easy way to analyze your financial portfolio. You can obtain a complimentary basic financial analysis by entering 9 bits of contact and financial information.

This analysis can help determine if you are on track for a successful retirement or if you may come up short. If you find the analysis doesn't match your desired results, contact me to see if I could provide recommendations that may help you attain your financial goals and improve your retirement picture.

To get started now; visit **www.jimsloan.com** and click the orange ***Retirement Analyzer*** button.

About the Author

Jim E. Sloan is the founder of Jim Sloan & Associates, LLC, a comprehensive wealth management firm located in Highlands Ranch, Colorado. Jim is an Investment Adviser Representative of AE Wealth Management, LLC, an SEC Registered Investment Adviser. This relationship allows Jim Sloan & Associates, LLC to bring institutional-level experience, practices, and pricing to individual families. Jim is also a licensed insurance agent. This is Jim's sixth financial book and is aimed at helping investors become financially informed.

Jim is a U.S. Army veteran, native Houstonian, and lives on the Front Range in the Denver area, volunteers with several charities, believes in the name of Jesus, loves to travel, and enjoys most things outdoors.

Made in the USA
Monee, IL
04 November 2026

67378677R00056